A Guide for Using

Hatchet

in the Classroom

Based on the novel written by Gary Paulsen

This guide written by **Donna Ickes and Edward Sciranko**

Teacher Created Resources, Inc.
6421 Industry Way
Westminster, CA 92683
www.teachercreated.com
ISBN: 978-1-55734-449-6
©*1994 Teacher Created Resources, Inc.*
Reprinted, 2008
Made in U.S.A.

Edited by
Walter Kelly

Illustrated by
Keith Vasconcelles

Cover Art by
Nancee McClure

Table of Contents

Introduction

Good books are wonderful! They stimulate our imaginations, inform our minds, inspire our higher selves, and fill our time with magic! With good books, we are never lonely or bored. And a good book only gets better with time, because each reading brings us new meaning. Each new story is a treasure to cherish forever.

In *Literature Units*, we take great care to select books that will become treasured friends for life.

Teachers using this unit will find the following features to supplement their own valuable ideas.

- Sample Lesson Plans

- Pre-reading Activities

- A Biographical Sketch and Picture of the Author

- A Book Summary

- Vocabulary Lists and Suggested Vocabulary Activities

- Chapters grouped for study, with sections including:

    - *quizzes*

    - *hands-on projects*

    - *cooperative learning activities*

    - *cross-curriculum connections*

    - *extensions into the readers' lives*

- Post-reading Activities

- Book Report Ideas

- Research Ideas

- A Culminating Activity

- Three Different Options for Unit Tests

- Bibliography

- Answer Key

We are confident that this unit will be a valuable addition to your literature planning, and that as you use our ideas, your students will learn to treasure the stories to which you introduce them.

Sample Lesson Plan

Lesson 1
- Introduce and complete some or all of the prereading activities. (page 5)
- Read "About the Author" with your students. (page 6)
- Read the book summary with your students. (page 7)
- Introduce the vocabulary list for Section 1. You may want to make sure that students can pronounce and define words when introduced. (page 8)

Lesson 2
- Read Chapters 1-4. Students may read in pairs, orally, or silently by themselves.
- Help students to understand the vocabulary words in this context.
- Play a vocabulary game. (page 9)
- Make a model glider. (page 11)
- Discuss the book in terms of health. (page 13)
- Construct an airplane setting. (page 12)
- Administer the Section 1 quiz. (page 10)
- Introduce the vocabulary list for Section 2. (page 8)

Lesson 3
- Read Chapters 5–8. Help students to understand the vocabulary words in this context.
- Play a vocabulary game. (page 9)
- Find out about bears. (page 19)
- Discuss the airplane's flight in terms of math. (page 18)
- List the items needed for survival. (page 17)
- Make a model of the camp. (page 16)
- Administer the Section 2 quiz. (page 15)
- Introduce the vocabulary list for Section 3. (page 8)

Lesson 4
- Read Chapters 9–12. Help students to understand the vocabulary words in this context.
- Play a vocabulary game. (page 9)
- Make Backwoods Tracker Cards. (page 21)
- Talk about Brian's luck and produce comic strips. (page 22)

- Discuss the book and science. (page 23)
- Find out about fire safety. (page 24)
- Administer the Section 3 quiz. (page 20)
- Introduce the vocabulary list for Section 4. (page 8)

Lesson 5
- Read Chapters 13–16. Help students to understand the vocabulary words in this context.
- Play a vocabulary game. (page 9)
- Interview the moose and write his news story. (page 28)
- Gather and share information about tornadoes. (page 29)
- Share parts of the book aloud. (page 27)
- Make a mobile. (page 26)
- Administer the Section 4 quiz. (page 25)
- Introduce the vocabulary list for Section 5. (page 8)

Lesson 6
- Read Chapters 17–Epilogue. Help students to understand the vocabulary words in this context.
- Play a vocabulary game. (page 9)
- Investigate exotic foods. (page 34)
- Design a Tee Shirt. (page 31)
- Present a play. (page 32)
- Discuss the book and literary characterizations. (page 33)
- Administer Section 5 quiz. (page 30)

Lesson 7
- Discuss Brian's later life. (page 35)
- Assign a book report and research project. (pages 36–37)
- Begin work on culminating activity. (pages 38–41)

Lesson 8
- Administer Unit Tests: 1, 2, and/or 3. (pages 42–44)
- Discuss the test answers and possibilities. (pages 46–48)
- Discuss the student's enjoyment of the book.
- Provide a list of related reading for your students.

Before the Book

Before you begin the book *Hatchet*, you can help students to recall background information and stimulate interest by completing the following activities and discussing some of the questions.

1. Study the book cover thoughtfully. What parts do you think that a hatchet might play in this story? Why did the illustrator choose this picture? What are you expecting this story to be about?

2. What other books by Gary Paulsen have you read? Do you expect that this storyline will be similar?

3. Have you ever been to the Canadian north woods or any other wooded area? What was it like? What did you like best?

4. Have you ever flown in a small plane? If so, describe the experience.

5. Are you a person who enjoys being outdoors? Do you like hunting and fishing? What other outdoor activities do you participate in?

6. Do you like to read about . . .

   • ways to survive in the woods?

   • realistic situations?

   • stories set in modern times?

7. How desperate would your circumstances have to be, before you would eat your food raw?

8. Have you ever had an experience where your life was in danger? If you have, you may want to share this experience with the class.

9. In groups, discuss the following:

   •What do you consider to be a dangerous situation?

   •Where would your story take place?

   •What kind of person could survive it?

   •How would he/she do this?

   •Work as a group to tell your own realistic tale of survival.

About the Author

Gary Paulsen was born in Minnesota in 1939 and still lives there part of the time with his wife, Ruth, and their son, Jim. He was raised by his grandmothers and his aunts, saying later with complete honesty, "My parents drank. They fought and drank and fought and drank. So I would hide in the basement—behind the furnace, in an old stuffed chair—and read." Although he has written more than 90 books and led his own life of adventure, Paulsen was not a good student and got through high school with difficulty. He attended Bemidji College for a short while, and then decided to join the army. These were only the beginnings of his search for an occupation he could live with; at different times he tried farming, ranching, trapping, professional archery, acting as a movie extra, tracking satellites, driving a truck, teaching school, and probably a lot of other things—until finally he became a magazine editor and then a writer. He says that writing is "all there is."

Since he draws deeply on his own experiences, relating them sometimes years later in a short story or book, it is obvious that Paulsen lives a life that is rich in adventure. In his book *Woodsong*, an autobiographical account of his relationships with his dog team and the outdoors, he states,

> *Most of my life it seems I've been in the forest or on the sea. Most of my time, sleeping or waking, has been spent outside, in close contact with what we now call the environment, what my uncle used to call simply, the woods.*

His adventures in "the woods" include running that dog team in the grueling Alaskan race, the Iditerod, which covers more than 1,180 miles of wilderness.

He is the author of hundreds of articles, short stories, and a few plays but is best known for his novels for young adults. His three Newbery Honor Books are *The Winter Room, Hatchet,* and *Dogsong.*

If you enjoy reading about Brian Robeson's experiences in *Hatchet,* you may want to continue reading about him in Paulsen's sequel, *The River,* in which an older Brian returns to the north woods. If you would like to know more about Gary Paulsen himself, read *Woodsong.*

Hatchet

by Gary Paulsen

(Puffin Books, 1988)

(Available in Canada from Penguin; UK, Penguin Books; AUS, Penguin Ltd.)

When Brian Robeson's plane goes down in the Canadian north woods after the pilot of the small bushplane dies of a heart attack, Brian, a "city boy," must learn to survive, even as he struggles with the pain of his parents' divorce and the secret he keeps about it.

Brian survives his injuries from the wreck, the onslaught of the hordes of mosquitoes, the sunburn, and the initial thirst and hunger, as he waits to be rescued. Within a few days, he finds shelter and his only food—some bitter berries that he gorges upon. These berries he later comes to call "gutcherries" because they cause him severe stomach pain. The boy grows in the ways of the woods as he finds raspberries, ignoring the bear that also comes to feast. He cannot ignore the porcupine, though, that stumbles into his shelter, perhaps looking for the store of berries that Brian has. He is injured once again, and after pulling the porcupine quills out of his leg, has a dream.

In this dream, Brian's father points to the fire that he is cooking on. When Brian awakes, he remembers the sparks that flew when he threw the precious hatchet against the rock wall. Thinking about this leads to the re-discovery of fire, and Brian's adjustment to the wilderness as he subsequently discovers turtle eggs and later, how to fish with bow and arrow. When he misses the attention of the pilot of a passing plane, however, he becomes deeply depressed and attempts suicide. Out of this despair comes a new confidence in himself and his power to survive, whether or not he is rescued.

Encounters with a skunk, a moose, and a tornado only deepen this confidence, and Brian decides to visit the sunken plane, hoping to recover the survival pack stowed in the fuselage. The survival pack yields precious dehydrated food and a transmitter that Brian discards after he assumes it is useless. The "broken" transmitter results in his rescue and his return to his mother.

The epilogue catalogs the changes in Brian due to his ordeal. It also recounts his adjustment to life as it had been, before his fifty-four days in the wilderness.

Vocabulary Lists

Section 1
(Chapters 1–4)

abated	altimeter	arc	banked	coma
consuming	depress	frustration	grimacing	hordes
hurtling	initial	intervals	keening	massive
rudder	slewed	spasm	turbulence	muck

Section 2
(Chapters 5–8)

amphibious	apparent	asset	crude	digital
diminish	gestures	interlaced	jets	lushly
motivated	pulverized	receded	relative	rivulets
ruefully	segment	seepage	stranded	gingerly

Section 3
(Chapters 9–12)

assumed	chamber	comprised	convulse	crest
depression	dormant	eddied	exasperation	flailing
focus	gnarled	gratified	haunches	intervals
motive	persistent	primitive	tendrils	tinder

Section 4
(Chapters 13–16)

camouflage	confines	corrosive	detach	devastating
exulted	fashioned	fragile	hummock	impaired
infuriating	prospect	punky	rectify	refracts
sarcasm	stabilize	unduly	virtual	precise

Section 5
(Chapters 17–Epilogue)

appetizer	drone	frenzied	furor	fuselage
incessant	momentary	murky	oblivious	predators
rummaging	stable	stymied	substantial	unwittingly

Vocabulary Activity Ideas

Students can begin with the contextual vocabulary from *Hatchet* and build upon it to use strategies for retaining, using, and extending their knowledge of word meanings. You may find some of these activities useful:

1. Have students illustrate the vocabulary words on one side of a sheet of paper. The word is written on the back. These can be used as a "quiz show" for a whole class activity, with one student acting as moderator, or they can be placed on a bulletin board or hallway display with the words added at the bottom. As a variation, students may do impromptu drawings on the chalkboard, challenging classmates to guess the word.

2. Language experience is fun at any age. Give each student a card with one of the vocabulary words on it. Allow a few minutes of "think time" for him/her to make up a sentence using that vocabulary word correctly. If you are teaching plot sequence, you may direct students to concentrate on retelling the narrative; for an enrichment activity, students could be given a general topic and an idea of sequence for an original story. It helps to tape responses for later transcription or student dictation.

3. Help students to experiment with word histories. Discuss specific words with the class, ones that you know contain foreign language roots. Make sure that these words have at least eight related words in the dictionary. Explain that related words use a common root but differ in their prefixes or suffixes. Have students illustrate their expanded vocabulary using a word web.

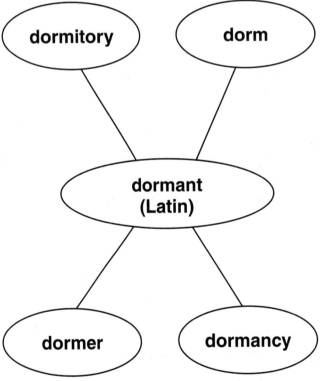

4. Play password. Have the group divide into two teams. Have vocabulary words already prepared, with each written on a 3" x 5" (7.5 cm x 12.5 cm) index card. One student from each team is to give clues using only one word and having a thirty-second time limit for response. Allow the student with the correct response to become the cluegiver, and keep score by allotting ten points for a correct answer on the first clue, nine points on the second clue, etc.

5. Use suffixes to teach grammar. Since many suffixes actually give clues to parts of speech, have students categorize words as usually a noun, verb, adjective, or adverb. For instance, a word that ends in -ment or -tion is usually a noun, a word that ends in -ly is usually an adverb, and a word that ends in -ed or -ing is usually either a verb or an adjective (participle). A little time spent with a dictionary may help students to apply grammar concepts more confidently and precisely.

6. Have students locate the vocabulary word in the story. Proceed to have them guess the meaning by using context clues.

Quiz Time

1. Who is Brian going to visit?

   _____

2. What is wrong with the pilot?

   _____

3. Why is Brian unable to say at first that the pilot is dead?

   _____

   _____

4. What will eventually happen if Brian just keeps the plane on a course pointing straight ahead?

   _____

   _____

5. Brian decides to fly the plane onto, and not into, the water. Explain the two choices and their consequences.

   _____

   _____

6. How does Brian indicate that he is finished talking on the radio and that he is ready to listen?

   _____

7. Why does Brian call the trees "the green death?"

   _____

8. Predict what would have happened to Brian if he had been knocked unconscious during the crash.

   _____

9. Brian is bothered by a secret that he is keeping. What is this secret?

   _____

10. Brian feels that he is both lucky and unlucky after the crash. How is he both lucky and unlucky?

   _____

Adventures in Aeronautics

Many of the aeronautics principles Brian encountered in his flight can be explored by making and flying a simple glider. You will need the following:

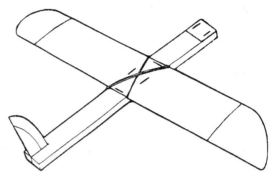

- Straight piece of light wood, such as balsa, 11" x 1" x ½" (28 cm x 2.54 cm x 1.3 cm)
- Stiff cardboard or poster board
- Stapler and staples
- Nylon thread
- Utility knife

Step 1: The piece of balsa wood is the fuselage. Cut a slit on the top that is 1¼" (3.12 cm) long; make sure that you cut it the whole way through to the bottom. This is for the tail fin.

Step 2: Cut the front and back wings and the tail from cardboard, as shown.

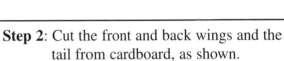

Step 3: Push the tail fin into the slot and secure it with staples.

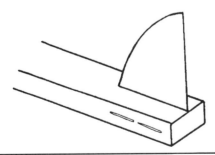

Step 4: Cut several small pieces that are ½" by 1" (1.3 cm x 2.5 cm) from the cardboard scraps. Fasten two of these to the front to elevate the nose. You may need the rest later, so keep them on hand.

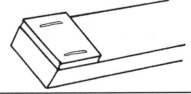

Step 5: Secure the wings as shown. First fasten them with staples and then wrap them with nylon thread.

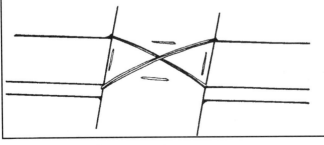

Step 6: Try your glider. You may need to add or subtract cardboard strips on the nose, change the position of the wings, or even experiment with a larger tail part. Decorating with insignia or numbers is optional but fun. And now, your mission is to complete a smooth glide of several feet. Good luck and good flying!

Authentic Settings

These first few chapters give you a sense of realism as Brian goes through the emotionally tense experience of the plane crash. As with any good drama, the authenticity of the setting adds to the intensity of the episode. Paulsen creates his setting by describing one object and then another as Brian's attention is focused on it. It is these details that add up to a complete visual picture in your mind. Let's make them even more real.

Divide into groups of three or four. Each person is to carefully re-read the episode to provide evidence about how the plane would look, inside and outside. Use the form below to keep a list of specific details marked *exterior* and look for such things as the model of the plane, the engine, the size, the gears and parts, and other aspects of the outside. Keep another list of details for the interior. Watch for instruments and details describing the cockpit.

Use your list of *exterior* details to help you make a drawing of the plane that Brian was in. You may want to go to the library to do some research. Present your complete drawing and your information to the class.

Using your list of details marked *interior,* create a mock-up of the cockpit of the plane. The library may be the best place to go for this kind of technical information. Folding cardboard panels salvaged from large boxes are excellent starting materials. You may want to make your mock-up full size so that you can actually sit in the pilot's seat as you explain the functions of the control panel to the class. If space is a problem, a smaller model may be a good choice.

Do you want to use your props further? Write a dialogue for Brian and the pilot, and perform this episode as a short play for your classmates or another group of students.

Exterior of Plane	Interior of Plane

Heart Connection

In the beginning chapters of *Hatchet*, the pilot suffers a fatal heart attack. Work with a partner to research the common warning signals of a heart attack. List them below.

1. _____

2. _____

3. _____

American Heart Association
National Center

According to the American Heart Association, 930,477 people died from cardiovascular disease in 1990. This was 43% of all deaths. For more information, contact the American Heart Association, 1-800-AHA-USA. They have special Getting to Know Your Heart kits available for educators.

There are ways to reduce the chances of heart disease. With your partner, find out what you can do to keep your heart healthy, both as a young person and as an adult. List some changes that you could make in your life now, to prevent heart problems later.

1. _____

_____

_____

2. _____

_____

_____

3. _____

_____

_____

4. _____

_____

_____

5. _____

_____

_____

Present this information to the class as a speech or a written report.

Swim for Your Life

But so Far! So far to the surface and his lungs could not do this thing, could not hold and were through, and he sucked water; took a great pull of water that would—finally—win, finally take him, and his head broke into light and he vomited and swam, pulling without knowing what he was, what he was doing. Pulling until his hands caught at weeds and muck, pulling ....

This is the dramatic description of Brian struggling to save his life, calling on all his strength and knowledge to survive. For most of us, swimming is considered fun, a sport. In reality, of course, it has always been a survival skill enabling humans from the dawn of history to cope with their environment.

Following are some basic kicks and strokes developed over the years.

The front crawl

The backstroke

The breaststroke

The butterfly

A. Research and carefully describe how each kick and stroke is performed. Include arm motion, leg motion, and breathing for each. You may cut out the above diagrams to illustrate your report.

B. Complete your report with a paragraph on water safety.

Quiz Time

1. Why does Brian feel that it is not so important that he does not know where he is, but that "they" do not know where he is?

   _____

2. What advice has Mr. Perpich, Brian's teacher, given Brian on attitude?

   _____

3. At the end of Chapter 5, Brian realizes that he needs to provide for two needs immediately if he is to survive. What are these two needs?

   _____

4. Brian's first attempt at building a fire fails. How does Brian try to start the first fire?

   _____

5. The site chosen by Brian for his shelter is described as a sideways bowl under a ledge. How does Brian think the bowl has been formed?

   _____

6. Explain how Brian is led to the berries.

   _____

7. When Brian sees his reflection in the water, it frightens him. What does Brian see when he looks at himself?

   _____

8. Even though Brian has seen the bear, he feels that it is safe to go back and pick berries. Why?

   _____

9. Brian shows that he has become more observant and thoughtful. What does Brian decide from the following observations?

   A. The clouds in the sky were scattered; therefore . . . _____

   B. It was breezy today, and therefore, there were no . . ._____

   C. If there was one kind of berry, then there must . . ._____

10. After being stuck by the porcupine, what does Brian decide is the most important rule of survival?

    _____

Modeling the Camp

An outdoorsman himself, Paulsen describes the shelter that Brian uses in practical detail, helping you to visualize both the interior and the exterior of the camp, along with its relative location along the lake.

Share your interpretation of Brian's shelter by making a model of what is eventually to become Brian's whole world. You may use your own modeling materials, or you may want to try sculpting with bread dough.

You will need the following materials:

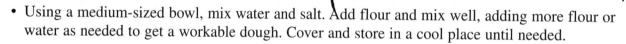

- 1¼ cups (300 mL) water
- 2 cups (480 mL) flour (Do not use the self-rising kind.)
- ½ cup salt (120 mL)
- Acrylic or poster paints and brushes
- Aluminum foil
- Cookie sheet
- Magic markers
- Polymer sealer

- Using a medium-sized bowl, mix water and salt. Add flour and mix well, adding more flour or water as needed to get a workable dough. Cover and store in a cool place until needed.

- Line a cookie sheet with aluminum foil. Using the magic marker, lay out the terrain of Brian's camp.

- Work the bread dough into the approximate shapes of the major forms that you will need.

- Bake in a 200° F (93° C) oven for 12 hours. You may now transfer your forms to a board or sturdy cardboard. Paint with acrylic paints and add details with magic markers, finishing with a coat of polymer sealer to preserve your work. Finally, add stones, dirt, sticks, or other natural items to complete your scene.

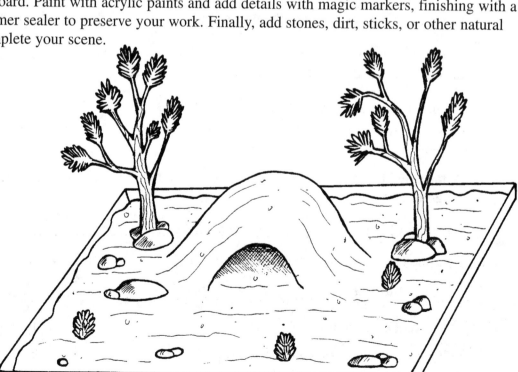

Items for Survival

In this segment of the book, Brian takes inventory of everything he owns, hoping to find some article that will be useful to him in his struggle for survival. Most of us, in a similar situation, would find that the commonplace articles that we always have with us would be of little use. Those who have experience in living in the outdoors, however, always have what they consider to be minimum survival equipment with them.

Divide into groups of three or four. Discuss the items that you would most like to have with you if you were stranded in the Canadian north woods. List them below. Following are the requirements:

- All items should be small enough to fit in your pockets.
- You are limited to a maximum of seven items.
- You may not include any communications devices in your list.
- You should remember that you will need tools to help you to survive for a long period of time, rather than temporary items such as food.

Survival Items

1. _____

2. _____

3. _____

4. _____

5. _____

6. _____

7. _____

When you are finished, prepare a short oral or written presentation for the class, explaining the reasons for your choices.

If several groups have completed this activity, each should present its inventory to the class for discussion. Remember, the idea is to survive!

Distance = Rate x Time

Until Brian remembered that the plane had flown off course before it crashed, he had hoped that the rescuers would find him quickly. He expected them to find him by using a mathematical formula that would tell them the approximate area in which the plane could be found. Since the pilot had filed a flight plan that told them the direction he would be traveling, they would be able to figure how far he could have traveled by using the formula: distance = rate x time.

For example: A plane flying north at 150 mph (rate) for 3 hours (time) will be 450 miles (distance) north of the airport. 150 x 3 = 450. (If using the metric system, simply substitute kilometers per hour for mph in the examples on this page.)

The formula can be changed to find rate or time if distance traveled is known and either the rate or time traveled.

For example:

$$\frac{distance}{time} = \text{rate}$$

$$\frac{distance}{rate} = \text{time}$$

See if you can correctly fill in the missing information in the chart.

Distance	Rate	Time
810 miles	_____ mph	15 hours
_____ miles	20 mph	6 hours
344 miles	_____ mph	8 hours
650 miles	65 mph	_____ hours
1545 miles	515 mph	_____ hours

Try these.

- If you are riding in a car that is going 55 mph, how soon will you reach a city that is 825 miles away? How much longer will you have to travel if you have to detour an additional 55 miles?

- If you travel 200 miles in 5 hours, and 150 miles in 2 more hours, what is the rate you travel for the whole trip?

What About Bears?

Bears, like other large wild animals, can be fascinating. We may think we know the characteristics of a bear like the one Brian saw, but do we really? For example, do you know how fast the black bear can run? Let's see what we really know. Write what you think the answers are to the following questions and then look up information in an encyclopedia to see how correct you were.

Bear Questions	What I Think	Correct Information
1. About how long does a black bear live?		
2. About how fast can a black bear run?		
3. About how long is a black bear?		
4. About how much does the average black bear weigh?		
5. What color is a black bear?		

Quiz Time

1. How does throwing his hatchet at the porcupine lead Brian to making his first fire?

   _____

   _____

2. Why does Brian feel that the fire is his friend?

   _____

   _____

3. How has Brian learned so much about turtles?

   _____

   _____

4. How does Brian solve the problem of not having a fire to cook the eggs?

   _____

5. How does Brian see and hear differently from when he first crashed into the lake?

   _____

6. Where does Brian plan to put his signal fire, and why does he choose that place?

   _____

7. Why, according to Brian, does he keep missing the fish?

   _____

   _____

8. What does Brian mean when he says, "discoveries happened because they needed to happen"?

   _____

9. What is it that blows up and away in a flurry of leaves and thunder?

   _____

10. Not being rescued by the plane that flew over has what effect on Brian?

   _____

   _____

Backwoods Tracker Cards

Brian came across some very unusual tracks—a main center line with claw marks to the side. Later, he discovered that the animal which made them was a turtle. As Brian became more skilled at looking and understanding, he probably learned to recognize many wild animal tracks near the lake. Some of these may have included the ruffed grouse, the moose, the bear, and the porcupine. Following are pictures of six animals and six tracks.

A. Cut these out, mount them on tagboard squares, and write a clear set of directions for a matching game of your invention.

B. For your game, research, locate, and add pictures and tracks for four more animals of the Canadian north woods.

C. Pack your directions and all 20 tracker cards into an old shoe box or other small gift box which you may cover, decorate appropriately, and label with your own title and illustrations.

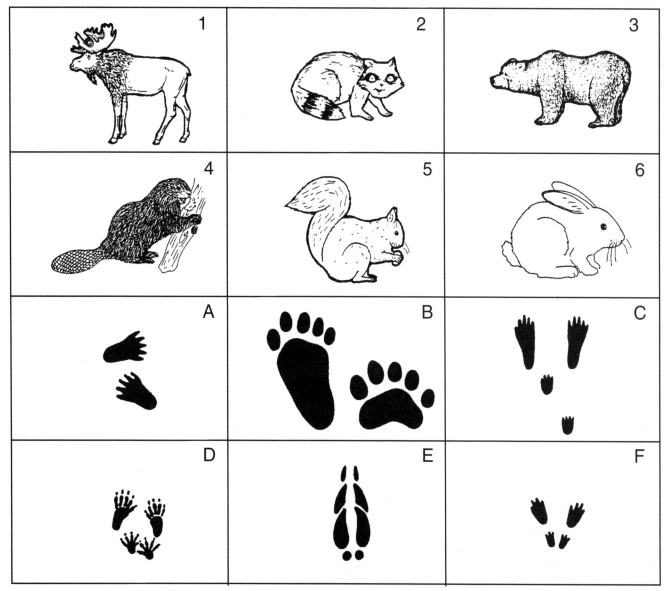

More Than Luck

Brian says that his survival is dependent upon luck more than anything else, and in many instances, this has been true. However, he is beginning to realize that his past experiences, such as the things that he was taught in school or remembers from movies, have helped him. Too, he is beginning to turn into a true woodsman—he is observing, really seeing what is around him and forming a new way of thinking.

In groups of five, discuss Brian's survival so far. Label major events as luck, past knowledge, or new knowledge. A chart such as this may help you.

Luck	New Knowledge	Past Knowledge

When your group is finished, share your information with the class by illustrating one of these events with a five-frame comic strip. After the group agrees upon a sequence of pictures and dialogue, each member should prepare one frame for the final product.

Finished comic strips, especially colorful ones, make great bulletin board displays!

What Makes Fires?

Brian has to rely on what he has learned in school, while playing, watching television, and observing what is around him. One of the things that Brian has learned about is the conditions that are needed for a fire. List the three things Brian knew he needed for a fire and explain what each term means. If necessary, look it up in an encyclopedia.

1. _____

_____

2. _____

_____

3. _____

_____

Think about the two ways Brian tried to make fire and how he needed all three of the conditions you listed. Describe the two attempts, explaining what conditions (if any) might have been lacking.

_____

_____

_____

_____

Why do you think he was unable to make fire by rubbing the sticks together?

_____

_____

_____

_____

_____

_____

_____

Fire — Friend or Foe?

Fire is a friend to all of us. It keeps us warm, cooks our food, gives us light, and does many other things. Fire can also be our foe when it is not controlled, destroying us and our belongings. One way to keep fire as a friend is to be careful with it and to take steps to keep it under control. With this purpose in mind, make a fire safety check of your home. Some things to look for are listed below.

- **Frayed wires on appliances**
- **Piles of used rags**
- **Flammable items near stoves, and fireplaces**
- **Smoke detectors (fresh batteries?)**
- **A fire escape plan that everyone knows**
- **Emergency phone numbers easy to find**
- **Fire extinguisher in kitchen and near fireplaces, etc.**

Make a list of any fire safety problems that need attention in your home. In the second column write the date that the problem was taken care of.

Fire Safety Problem	Date Problem Was Solved

Quiz Time

1. What two true things come to Brian's mind after not being rescued by the plane?

   _____

2. Explain how Brian's first bow nearly spells disaster for him.

   _____

   _____

3. Why is Brian not able to hit the fish with his arrows?

   _____

   _____

4. What does Brian learn is the most important thing that drives all creatures in the forest?

   _____

5. What does Brian decide his shelter should provide in addition to keeping out the wind and rain?

   _____

6. Brian needs a ladder so that he can safely store his food. From what and how does he make a ladder?

   _____

7. Minutes and hours are meaningless to Brian as a measure of time. How does Brian measure time?

   _____

8. What does Brian learn he is doing wrong in the way he is trying to kill a foolbird?

   _____

9. What animal attacks Brian at the lake and nearly kills him?

   _____

10. How does Brian react to being attacked and nearly killed at the lake, and then having everything destroyed by a tornado?

    _____

    _____

Make a Mobile

A mobile is perfect for illustrating groups or clusters of ideas. Make yours eye-catching by paying attention to color and shape as well as ideas, and you will have a display that can transform a room!

Titles for your mobiles might include *Mistakes, First Days, How to Improve a Shelter, or Survival Rules.* You may have a few ideas of your own that you want to use, too.

For this project you will need the following:

- A list of concepts to illustrate

- A paper plate

- Yarn, string, or ribbon

- Cardboard or posterboard

- Markers or paints

- A dowel about 8" (20 cm) long, or an unsharpened pencil.

1. Using your list and the posterboard or cardboard, draw each item for your mobile.

2. Paint or color the items. As you cut them out, be aware of the shape, or silhouette, of each example. This will be the first thing your audience will notice about your mobile.

3. Cut a length of string or ribbon about 18" (46 cm) long. Attach one end of it to the center of the pencil or dowel by wrapping it a few times around and securing it with a knot.

4. Make a small hole in the center of the paper plate. Thread the free end of the string through the hole in the center of the paper plate and pull it through, drawing the dowel or pencil tightly against the plate. Tie a knot in the upper end of the string. This step will provide support for your items and will also make a stronger hanger for your finished work.

5. Again using string or ribbon and a needle, attach the parts of the mobile to the outside rim of the paper plate. Make sure that your items are balanced properly so that the finished project does not lean to one side.

6. Use the knotted end of the string to suspend your mobile, allowing it to move freely.

Let Me Share the Part Where . . .

Everyone has a favorite part in the book—a paragraph or a few sentences which make you smile or wince, or in some way, react personally to feel that you really understand what the author means. This segment of the book describes big changes in Brian as he begins to understand himself and how he fits in with his environment. He finally knows "two true things," he would not let death in, and he was not the same as he had been. This turning point in the story leads us to understand why Paulsen wrote the novel. It gives us the author's viewpoint of a real "hero."

What kind of person is Brian now? How can you tell? Is he someone you admire? Why?

In groups of two or three, discuss your reactions to these questions. Then find the particular passages that you feel support your ideas. Re-read them with the group and discuss why you find that these sentences or paragraphs reveal the "real Brian." Practice reading these excerpts with expression so that you can share them. Just to make sure that everyone gets the point of your discussion, in the box below paraphrase or summarize the sentences for your classmates.

Some quotations that you might want to begin with are these:

He knew the wolf now, as the wolf knew him, and he nodded to it, nodded and smiled.

Tough hope, he thought that night. I am full of tough hope.

And the last thought he had that morning as he closed his eyes was: I hope the tornado hit the moose.

_____

_____

_____

_____

_____

_____

_____

_____

Read All About It!

A newspaper article relies on answering questions that begin with who, what, where, when, why, and sometimes how. Pretend that you are the moose that attacked Brian. You have been interviewed by a news reporter to get your side of the incident at the lake. Use your imagination to create answers to the questions below. Then write the article as you think the reporter would. Remember, a good news story starts with an eye-catching title. When finished, copy it as it would appear in the newspaper.

Who? _____

What? _____

Where? _____

When? _____

Why? _____

How? _____

The Canadian Woods Daily

_____

_____

_____

_____

_____

_____

_____

_____

_____

_____

Knowledge Is Power

Brian is almost killed, and his shelter and belongings are destroyed by a tornado. Tornadoes are common in the United States; in fact, they are more common in the United States than any other place. Every year people are killed, and property is destroyed by tornadoes. Little or nothing can be done to save property from being destroyed, but lives can be saved if people have knowledge about tornadoes and what to do if they are in one. Gather information about tornadoes and answer the following questions. An additional activity would be to collect pictures of tornadoes and their destruction, or to draw a picture showing a tornado.

1. What is a tornado?

   _____

   _____

2. How fast are the winds inside a tornado spinning?

   _____

   _____

3. How wide can a tornado be at the ground?

   _____

   _____

4. In simple terms, how is a tornado created?

   _____

   _____

5. In what two ways does a tornado cause damage to property?

   _____

   _____

6. About how fast does a tornado travel across the ground?

   _____

   _____

7. According to the weather experts, what should you do if a tornado comes? Include ideas for being in different locations such as in your home, in the open, or in a car.

   _____

   _____

Quiz Time

1. Why does Brian want to go out to the plane?

   _____

2. What does Brian build so that he can get things from the plane to the shore?

   _____

3. How does Brian manage to get into the plane since there are no doors above the water?

   _____

4. Explain what Brian means when he says that the loss of the hatchet means that he has nothing?

   _____

5. How does Brian figure that the lake is not as deep as the plane is long?

   _____

6. What does Brian fear the plane might do while he is inside it?

   _____

7. List the items that are contained in the survival bag.

   _____

8. Brian says that the rifle and the matches change him and he is not sure if he likes the change. What change is he talking about, and why does he question the change it makes in him?

   _____

   _____

9. What does Brian accidentally do that results in his being rescued?

   _____

   _____

10. How has Brian changed as a result of his ordeal?

   _____

Design a Tee

If Brian were to look back over his experiences of the last fifty-four days, he would probably be able to sum up the lessons of his ordeal very concisely, maybe even cleverly. Many times, the mottos printed on tee shirts become trends in fashion because they seem to express a philosophy that many people can understand, while also being concise and clever.

Could you design a tee shirt that would make people stop and think for just a moment, or perhaps smile? You may want to use very few words, or many. You might decide to use one of your favorite quotations from the story. You may feel that a picture would add just the right touch to your creation, or you may concentrate on artistic printing. Whatever your design may turn out to be, you will need the following materials for this project:

- 1 tee shirt, preferably white or light-colored
- 1 box ordinary crayons
- an electric iron, with a portable ironing board
- 1 piece of cardboard, approximately 12" x 15" (30 cm x 38 cm)
- waxed paper

1. Draw your design on ordinary paper, making it the approximate size that will fit on your tee shirt. Remember, all print should be reversed, like a mirror image.

2. Now check to make sure that it will fit on your shirt. The design should not extend too close to the shoulders, or too low on the shirt, since it may be worn tucked in.

3. Color your design. Make sure that you have a strong layer of color in each area because light applications of crayon are usually not satisfactory.

4. Put the piece of cardboard inside the tee shirt. This will form a barrier so that your color does not bleed through to the back of the garment.

5. Cover your design with waxed paper and iron, using a moderate heat setting. If you need to check your work to see if the color has transferred, lift only a tiny corner. Do not allow the iron to rest too long in one area.

6. The finished product will be hand washable.

Play Time

Brian's rescue is low key, almost ordinary and commonplace. This ending is in direct contrast to the panic and excitement Brian showed in the first chapters of the book when his plane went down. Perhaps you wrote dialogue for the pilot (page 12), producing a short play of the crash; now would be a good time to add the final act.

After deciding upon the appropriate place to start your Act III, write the dialogue for Brian and his rescuer. Plan props and settings for your play. Assign parts to classmates, remembering that you will need a stagehand and perhaps a narrator and a director.

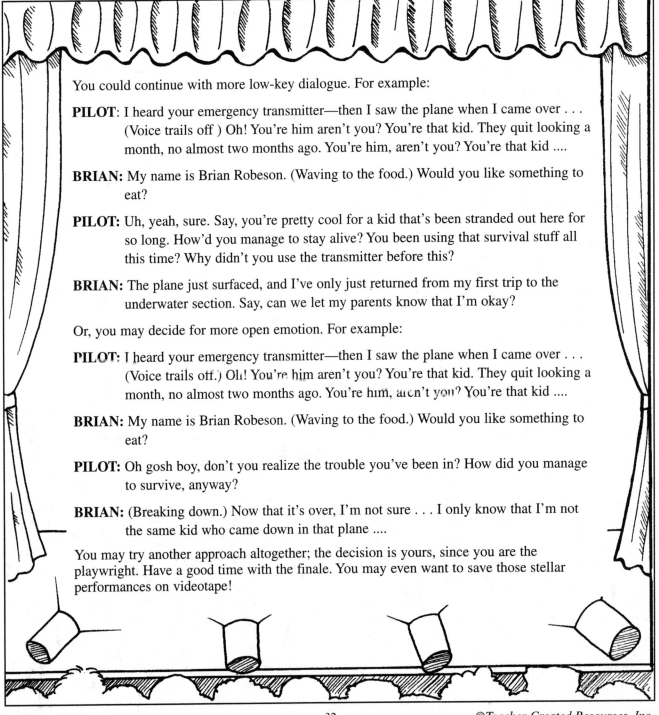

You could continue with more low-key dialogue. For example:

PILOT: I heard your emergency transmitter—then I saw the plane when I came over . . . (Voice trails off) Oh! You're him aren't you? You're that kid. They quit looking a month, no almost two months ago. You're him, aren't you? You're that kid ....

BRIAN: My name is Brian Robeson. (Waving to the food.) Would you like something to eat?

PILOT: Uh, yeah, sure. Say, you're pretty cool for a kid that's been stranded out here for so long. How'd you manage to stay alive? You been using that survival stuff all this time? Why didn't you use the transmitter before this?

BRIAN: The plane just surfaced, and I've only just returned from my first trip to the underwater section. Say, can we let my parents know that I'm okay?

Or, you may decide for more open emotion. For example:

PILOT: I heard your emergency transmitter—then I saw the plane when I came over . . . (Voice trails off.) Oh! You're him aren't you? You're that kid. They quit looking a month, no almost two months ago. You're him, aren't you? You're that kid ....

BRIAN: My name is Brian Robeson. (Waving to the food.) Would you like something to eat?

PILOT: Oh gosh boy, don't you realize the trouble you've been in? How did you manage to survive, anyway?

BRIAN: (Breaking down.) Now that it's over, I'm not sure . . . I only know that I'm not the same kid who came down in that plane ....

You may try another approach altogether; the decision is yours, since you are the playwright. Have a good time with the finale. You may even want to save those stellar performances on videotape!

Characterizations

An important benefit of reading literature is to learn more about how people act. We can also learn about why they act the way they do. This information can also help you understand yourself better.

The way we decide about a person's character in a story is basically the same as it is in real life. A person is judged by what he says, does, or by what others say about him. In a story, we can sometimes also know what a person is thinking.

As a group or individually, list the traits that you feel would best describe Brian's character. To support your point of view, think of some of the things Brian said, did, or thought that demonstrate the traits you have listed.

Trait	Proof
_____	_____
_____	_____
_____	_____
_____	_____

A character may also be described as being dynamic or static. A dynamic character is one who changes as the story progresses. A static character remains the same throughout the story. Decide if you think Brian was a static or dynamic character and give specific examples to demonstrate your point of view.

_____

_____

_____

_____

_____

What's for Dinner?

After returning to civilization, Brian is fascinated by food. He stops in grocery stores and stares at the aisles of food.

Visit a grocery store and make a list of foods you have never eaten. Pay particular attention to exotic foods like octopus, escargots, or caviar. List some of the new foods you discovered in the boxes below. For each, write a very short description or draw a picture of the food.

Food	*Food*
Food	*Food*
Food	*Food*

A fun activity for the whole family would be to plan and prepare a meal together. It would be especially interesting to include some of the exotic foods that you have never eaten before and would like to try.

Brian's Later Life

When you have finished reading Hatchet, you may feel so familiar with Brian, a fictional character, that you would like to know about his "later life." Since imaginary characters have no boundaries, you may want to add details to Brian's adult years. On the lines below, write any questions you want answered about Brian's later life.

_____

_____

_____

Alone or in groups, write your own original answers for your questions. Consider other things, too, such as the following:

• Does Brian ever return to the woods where he spent his ordeal? _____

• How do the kids treat Brian after he returns to school? _____

• Do Brian and his mother get along better? _____

• Does Brian go to college? If he does, what does he study? If not, how does he make a living?

• Does Brian get married? Does he have children? Does he share his adventure with them, or keep silent?

   _____

• What does Brian say to Perpich when he sees him again? _____

• Construct a time line of Brian's life, beginning with his rescue and ending at age fifty. When you are finished, share your time line with your classmates.

   _____

Book Report Ideas

Preparing a book report does not have to be tedious, as the list of alternatives below should show you. You may decide to use one of the ideas below for your report on Hatchet, or you may choose another method that interests you.

Write a Poem: You may want to use some of the vocabulary words that you have learned as you read, or you may want to create more freely; see if you can capture the spirit of the book in your poem. Remember, poems do not have to rhyme.

Design a New Book Cover: If you would like to try your hand at creating a new cover, now is your chance. Do not forget to use the space on the front and back flaps to add information to your project.

Character Diary: Choose several important days at strategic points throughout the book. Write diary entries that Brian might have written if he had kept a diary.

Diorama: Create a diorama. This is a miniature scene, using dried or living plants, stones, dirt, small figures, and background pictures, etc., to create a three-dimensional effect. This is an excellent project for stories set outdoors.

Character Puppet or Doll: Bring a character to life, using materials you have at home, or re-cycle old materials to make a puppet or a doll.

Collage: Browse through magazines, looking for illustrations that remind you of situations that you have read about in the novel. Cut and paste these illustrations on a sheet of art paper. Or, generate images on a computer or draw them yourself. Adding quotations from the story may complete your project.

Be a Critic: Pretend that you are a famous book critic, giving his/her opinion of the book on a television news show. Write a script for yourself, add props, and you are ready to go.

Design a Comic Book: Choose a chapter or an episode from the book that is especially alive for you, and illustrate it as a comic book. Include "balloons" for characters' conversations or thoughts.

Do a One-Woman/Man Show: Dress as one of the characters in the book. Prepare a monologue for your performance in which the character speaks to the audience about his/her feelings or experiences.

Research Ideas

List three things from *Hatchet* that you would like to know more about.

1. _____

2. _____

3. _____

In *Hatchet,* Paulsen drew on his years of experience to paint a realistic picture of Brian's days in the woods. He described wildlife and their habitat, survival techniques, airplanes, and the Canadian woods. He also used several scientific principles. Build your knowledge in these areas and increase your understanding of the novel and its author by researching any of the following:

- The geography and geology of the Canadian north woods

- The trees and plants of the Canadian north woods

- The wildlife of Canada, particularly the following:

    foolbirds

    kinds of fish

    moose

    porcupines

    skunks

    wolves

    turtles

- Wilderness survival methods, including the following:

    finding or building shelter

    finding food

    making fires

    setting up a safe camp

    fighting insects

    making weapons

- Airplanes

    history of the small plane

    Cessna 406

    bushplanes and their pilots

When you are finished, present your new knowledge to the class orally. You may add illustrations if you wish.

Survival Fair Planning

The time that Brian spent in the woods changed his life. He had to learn to depend on himself; he had to learn to find his own food; and he had to stay strong and uninjured. By reading about his experiences, you may have grown in survival skills, too.

To celebrate the successful end of *Hatchet*, plan a Survival Fair for your classmates and other invited guests. This fair could have booths, displays, and contests of skill. Any fair needs to be planned in detail for smooth operation. The sheet below will help you.

Plans for Survival Fair

Food Booths (Possibilities include dehydrated or exotic foods as well as chocolate "mousse" and "porcupine" hors d'oeuvres, etc.)

1. _____
2. _____
3. _____

Performance Booths (You may want to include some of the sets that you have constructed or the scenes that you have written. You could present live or video-taped performances of "The Crash" or "The Rescue," as well as dramatic readings from the book.)

1. _____
2. _____
3. _____

Displays (Include all of the projects that you have made during your reading of *Hatchet*. Examples are tee shirts, model gliders, etc.)

1. _____
2. _____
3. _____

Contests of Skill (Include as many of your own ideas here as you can.)

1. _____
2. _____

Survival Fair Food Booths

You may have already planned a good many food booths for your fair, but you may want to include these items, considering the problems that Brian had with each animal.

"Porcupine" Hors D'oeuvres

- 1 lb. (453.6 g) ground beef
- 1 15 oz. (450 mL) can tomato sauce
- ¼ cup (60 mL) uncooked rice
- 1 tsp. (5 mL) Worcestershire sauce
- ⅓ cup (80 mL) minced onion
- 1 egg
- ½ cup (120 mL) water
- salt and pepper to taste

Mix 4 tablespoons (60 mL) of the tomato sauce with the egg, and then stir in the rice, onion, salt and pepper, and ground beef. Make into little balls and fry. Combine the remaining tomato sauce with Worchestershire sauce and water. Add the cooked meatballs. Bring to a boil, and then simmer on low heat for a least one-half hour.

Layered Chocolate "Mousse"

Mix and press into a 9" x 13" (22.5 cm x 32.5 cm) pan:

- 1 cup (240 mL) flour
- ½ cup (120 mL) chopped nuts
- ½ cup (120 mL) soft butter
- Bake at 350° F (180° C) for 15 minutes. Cool.

Blend together and spread over the first layer:

- 8 oz. (240 mL) cream cheese
- 1 cup (240 mL) confectioners sugar
- 1 cup (240 mL) packaged whipped cream

Combine and spread on top:

- 2 small packages instant chocolate pudding made according to directions

Survival Fair Obstacle Course

Contestants in this competition will be both timed and judged. The winners will be the contestants with the fastest times after penalty seconds have been subtracted. A contestant must complete all stations in the obstacle course.

Materials needed to set up the course:

- Stopwatch
- Rope
- Two planks 8' (2.5 m) long, 2" (5 cm) thick, and 6" (15 cm) wide
- Stepladder
- Marker cones
- Cement blocks

Station One: Contestants are to climb to the fourth step on the ladder. A penalty of one second is added if the task is not completed properly.

Station Two: While on the fourth step of the ladder the contestant is to take the rope provided and to swing to the other side of a hazard. The hazard may be a rope circle, wading pool, mud puddle, etc. Falling into the hazard costs a one-second penalty.

Station Three: Contestants are to run through a maze of marker cones. Contestants must follow the marked course and not knock the cones over. Failure to go around a cone, or knocking a cone over, costs a penalty second for each offense.

Station Four: Contestants are to crawl under a set of five ropes. The ropes are to be about 18 in. (45 cm) above the ground and spaced about two feet (60 cm) apart. Touching a rope costs a one-second penalty.

Station Five: Contestants are to cross two planks that are placed about a foot off the ground. The first plank is to be crossed while walking forward. The second plank is to be crossed while walking backward. Each time you step off the plank, it costs one penalty second.

Station Six: The contestant must finish the course by hopping on one foot for about five yards (5 m) to the finish line. Touching the ground with the other foot or a hand costs one penalty second.

Scoring: One second is added to the student's time for each violation of the rules. The student with the fastest time is the survivor. Time keepers are needed to time the contestants, and judges are needed at each station to keep track of penalties.

Survival Fair—Reaction Wall

In Brian's shelter, he often thought about primitive humans, especially in terms of their discoveries of fire and the bow and arrow. Another aspect of cave living might be the freedom to write thoughts or sketch drawings on the walls.

You can offer this freedom to your classmates and invited guests by creating a "shelter wall" on one wall of your classroom, making a convenient area for thank-you notes and reactions to individual offerings at the fair. This is easily done by covering the wall with inexpensive shelf paper or butcher paper. (You may want to safeguard the wall beneath by providing several layers in case of bleedthrough). Attach pens, markers, or pencils at intervals, and invite your guests to write out their reactions to the fair. Have several student reactions already written on the wall so that guests understand. You may want to keep all or part of the Reaction Wall as a souvenir of your fair.

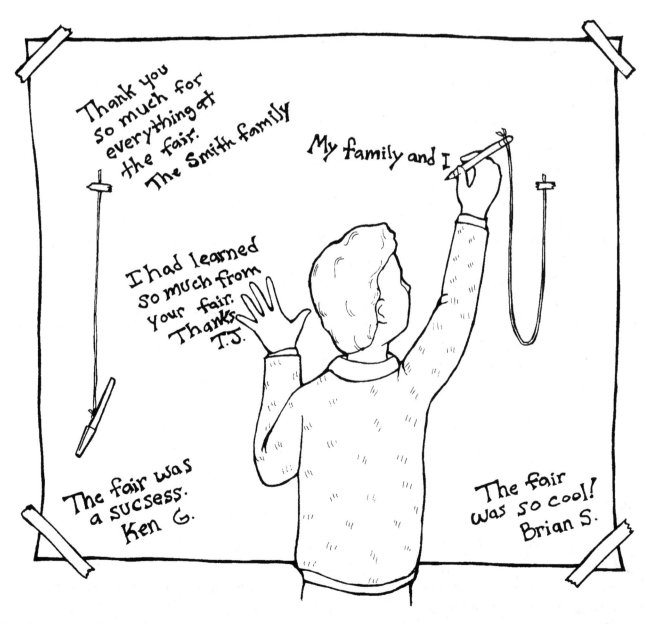

Objective Test and Essay

True or False: Answer true or false in the blanks below.

1. _____ Brian is going to visit his father for the summer.

2. _____ Mr. Perpich's advice is to stay calm and to wait for help to come.

3. _____ Brian feels his first most important need is a weapon for protection.

4. _____ Brian builds his first fire using his watch crystal.

5. _____ Brian relies on past experiences and knowledge to solve survival problems.

6. _____ Brian is scared away from the raspberries by a moose.

7. _____ Brian learns that self-pity is useless.

8. _____ Brian keeps the signal fire burning day and night.

9. _____ Brian is unable to spear the fish because they are too fast for him.

10. _____ Brian learns that nothing in nature can afford to be lazy.

Short Answer: Write a brief response to each question in the blank provided.

1. Why does Brian feel fire is his friend? _____

2. How does Brian's encounter with the porcupine illustrate that both good and bad can come from an incident? _____

3. Brian is almost blinded twice. How could becoming blind have been fatal to him? _____

4. How does Brian measure time while in the wilderness?_____

5. Why does Brian want to kill a foolbird when he now has all the fish he can eat?_____

6. Why is the pilot's flight plan useless to the searchers?_____

7. Why does Brian feel that he was foolish in thinking that the turtle had come ashore to play? _____

   _____

8. Brian learns that things happen fast. Give any two examples from the story that show this.

   _____

9. How is Brian able to get the items from the plane to the shore? _____

10. Which two items from the plane do you think Brian liked the most? _____

Essay: Respond to the following on the back of this paper.
Throughout the story Brian is faced by survival problem after survival problem. Think back to the story and pick any two events that you feel were the most exciting or interesting. Retell the event and then tell what made it special for you.

Test

Explain the meaning of each of these quotations from *Hatchet*.

Chapter 1:   *"He was alone. In the roaring plane with no pilot he was alone."*

Chapter 4:   *"If you keep walking back from good luck, he thought, you'll come to bad luck."*

Chapter 5:   *"People have gone for many days without food as long as they've got water. Even if they don't come close until late tomorrow I'll be all right."*

Chapter 7:   *"It frightened him—the face was cut and bleeding, swollen and lumpy, the hair all matted, and on his forehead a cut had healed but left the hair stuck with blood and scab."*

Chapter 8:   *"He did not know how long it took, but later he looked back on this time of crying in the corner of the dark cave and thought of it as when he learned the most important rule of survival, which was that feeling sorry for yourself just didn't work."*

Chapter 10:   *"I will not let you go out, he said to himself, to the flames—not ever."*

Chapter 11:   *"l am not the same, he thought. I see, I hear differently."*

Chapter 13:   *"The plane passing had changed him, the disappointment cut him down and made him new."*

Chapter 16:   *"He started to move, ever so slowly; her head turned and her back hair went up—like the hair on an angry dog—and he stopped, took a slow breath, the hair went down and she ate."*

Chapter 18:   *"Two hours, almost three he dragged and stumbled in the dark, brushing the mosquitoes away, sometimes on his feet, more often on his knees, finally to drop across the bag and to sleep when he made the sand in front of the doorway."*

Epilogue: *"For years after his rescue he would find himself stopping in grocery stores to just stare at the aisles of food, marveling at the quantity and the variety."*

Teacher Note: Choose an appropriate number for your students.

Conversations

Work in groups to write and perform the conversations that might have occurred in each of the following situations.

- Brian is riding to the airport with his mother. She keeps trying to get him to talk, but he does not want to. *(2 people)*

- The judge asks Brian where he wants to live, questions his parents, and grants their divorce. *(4 people)*

- Brian and his friend Terry are riding their bikes near the mall when Brian sees his mother and The Secret. *(2 people)*

- Perpich teaches his class to "get motivated," and Brian responds with comments and questions. *(2 people)*

- Brian and his friend Terry are joking and making things up and pretending that they are lost in the woods. They discuss what they would do. *(2 people)*

- Over stew and peach whip, Brian and the pilot who rescues him discuss the days in the woods. *(2 people)*

- Brian's parents are told that he has been rescued. *(2 people)*

- Brian and his parents are back together, sitting at breakfast on the day after his return. *(3 people)*

- Brian and a group of his friends are talking on his first day back at school. *(2 or more people)*

Bibliography of Related Reading

Fiction

Aiken, Joan. *Midnight Is a Place.* Dell, 1985.

Ansell, Rod, and Rachel Percy. *To Fight the Wild.* HBJ, 1986.

Ashley, Bernard. *Break in the Sun.* S.E. Phillips, 1980.

Bawden, Nina. *Henry.* Lothrop, 1988.

Blackwood, Gary. *Wild Timothy.* Macmillan, 1987.

Blades, Ann. *Boy of Tache.* Tundra Books, 1973.

Defoe, Daniel. *Robinson Crusoe.* Macmillan, 1962.

Fleming, Susan. *Trapped on the Golen Flyer.* Westminster Press, 1978.

George, Jean Craighead. *Julie of the Wolves.* Harper Collins, 1974.

    My Side of the Mountain. Puffin, 1976.

    The Talking Earth. HarperCollins, 1989.

Hill, Kirpatrick. *Toughboy and Sister.* M.K. McElderry Books, 1990.

Morpurgo, Michael. *King of the Cloud Forests.* Viking, 1988.

O'Dell, Scott. *Black Pearl.* Houghton Mifflin, 1967.

    Black Star, Bright Dawn. Houghton Mifflin, 1988.

    Island of the Blue Dolphins. Dell, 1987.

Paterson, Katherine. *Bridge to Terabithia.* HarperCollins, 1977.

Paulsen, Gary. *Canyons.* Dell, 1991.

    The Crossing. Dell, 1990.

    Dancing Carl. Bradbury Press, 1983.

    Dogsong. Bradbury Press, 1985.

    The Island. Dell, 1990.

    The River. Doubleday, 1991.

    Sentries. Puffin, 1986.

    Tracker. Puffin, 1984.

    The Voyage of the Frog. Orchard Books Watts, 1989.

    The Winter Room. Orchard Books Watts, 1989.

Ross, Rhea. *The Bet's on Lizzie Bingmam.* Houghton & Mifflin, 1988.

Ruckman, Ivy. *Night of the Twisters.* HarperCollins, 1984.

Rylant, Cynthia. *A Blue-Eyed Daisy.* Bradbury, 1985.

Speare, Elizabeth. *The Sign of the Beaver.* Houghton Mifflin, 1983.

St. George, Judith. *In the Shadow of the Bear.* Berkley Books, 1983.

Swindells, Robert. *Brother in the Land.* Holiday House, 1984.

Taylor, Theodore. *The Cay.* Avon, 1969.

Nonfiction

Dalrymple, Byron. *Survival in the Outdoors.* Dutton, 1972.

George, Jean Craighead. *The Wild, Wild Cookbook.* Thomas Crowell, 1982.

Mooers, Robert L., Jr. *Finding Your Way in the Outdoors.* Outdoor Life Books, 1972.

Patent, Dorothy H. *Hunters and the Hunted.* Holiday House, 1981.

    The Way of the Grizzly. Clarion, 1987.

Riviere, Bill. *Backcountry Camping.* Dolphin Books, 1972.

Answer Key

Page 10

1. His father.
2. He died of a heart attack.
3. He was too afraid to admit it.
4. The plane will run out of gas and crash.
5. The surface of water is very hard, and a crash into it will be more severe than skidding on top of it.
6. He says "Over."
7. He knows that if he hits them, they will tear the plane apart.
8. He would have drowned.
9. His mother had a boyfriend and was cheating on his father.
10. He is lucky because he is alive, but he is unlucky because he is alone and lost in the wilderness.

Page 13

Warning Signs for a Heart Attack

1. Uncomfortable pressure, fullness, squeezing or pain in the center of the chest lasting more than two minutes.
2. Pain that spreads to the shoulders, neck, or arms.
3. Severe pain, lightheadedness, fainting, sweating, nausea or shortness of breath may also occur. (These signals are not always present, or sometimes they may subside and then return.)

Changes to Make:

1. Do not smoke. Your risk is doubled.
2. Control your blood pressure.
3. Control your cholesterol and fat intake with diet.
4. Exercise aerobically three times a week for a minimum of 20 minutes each time.
5. Control your weight with diet.
6. See your physician for diabetes testing.

Page 15

1. Brian is unable to get out to civilization, and the others do not know where to find him.
2. Be positive and get motivated was the message.
3. Basic needs are food and shelter.
4. Brian tried to start a fire by rubbing two sticks together.
5. A glacier had scooped out the bowl-shaped area.
6. The colors, sounds, and actions of the birds attracted Brian to the berries.
7. Brian's face was cut, bleeding, and swollen. His eyes were slits, and he was dirty.
8. Brian felt safe to return to the berries, because he felt that the bear had indicated that it did not mind sharing.
9. A. ... no rain.
   B. ... no mosquitoes
   C. ... must be more berries.
10. Brian learned that feeling sorry for himself did not work.

Answer Key (cont.)

Page 18

Distance divided by time equals rate.

Distance divided by rate equals time.

54 mph;

120 miles;

43 mph;

10 hours;

3 hours;

15 hours;

1 hour more

350 miles in 7 hours would be an average rate of 50 mph for the whole trip

Page 19

1. 15 to 30 years
2. 25 mph
3. 5ft.
4. 200 to 300 pounds
5. Black; rusty brown; cinnamon; white; a mix of gray and black.

Page 20

1. When the hatchet hit the rock, sparks were created. These sparks eventually caused Brian to think of using the sparks to create a fire.
2. Fire provides warmth, protection, and enables him to cook. (Answers may vary.)
3. Brian had learned about turtles from a television show.
4. Brian had to eat the eggs raw.
5. Brian has become more observant, and he carefully identifies things he comes in contact with.
6. The signal fire was to be on top of a ridge for better visibility.
7. Brian felt he was too slow to get the fish.
8. A need causes us to search for and to find an answer. (Answers may vary.)
9. The bird was a foolbird, or grouse.
10. Brian felt hopeless.

Page 23

1. oxygen. 2. fuel. 3. heat.

(Answers may vary in parts two and three.)

Page 25

1. Brian now knew two things. He had changed and would never be the same, and that he would live.
2. When it broke, the bow nearly blinded him, and blindness would have been fatal.
3. Water refracts light, causing the fish to appear to be in a different position than they really are.
4. Food was the center of everything in nature.
5. A shelter must provide protection.
6. A type of ladder was made by Brian cutting the branches off a pine tree to form steps.
7. Time came to be measured by important events.
8. Brian had not been able to get the birds until he realized that he had been looking for them in a wrong way. He learned to look for shapes and outlines instead of a full-colored bird.
9. A moose attacked Brian.
10. Brian was tough minded and was ready to accept any and all challenges to his survival.

Answer Key *(cont.)*

Page 29

1. A tornado is a violent, dark, spinning, funnel-shaped wind.
2. Winds (although not known for certain) are estimated to be between 200 and 400 mph (320-640 kmph).
3. The width of a tornado is from 10 ft. to 1,000 ft. (3m-300 m) and averages about 220 yards (210 m).
4. Tornadoes are caused when moist warm air is under dry cool air. The warm air rushes up, creating thunderstorms and sometimes tornadoes.
5. Damage is caused by the strong winds and also by a low-pressure area. When the air rushes in, it causes an explosive force.
6. Tornadoes move at 20 to 40 mph. (32-64 kmph) and average 30 mph (48 kmph).
7. Accept appropriate responses.

Page 30

1. Brian wanted to get to the plane for the survival pack.
2. Brian needed a raft to get to the plane and to get things back to shore.
3. The hatchet was used to chop an entry hole into the plane.
4. The hatchet was everything because it provided Brian with tools, food, and shelter.
5. Brian knew that the water was not as deep as the plane was long because it was in the water on an angle, and part of it was out of the water.
6. Brian feared that the plane might slip or sink under the water while he was inside.
7. From the plane, Brian got a sleeping bag, a sleeping pad, a cookset, matches, a lighter, a knife and compass, a first-aid kit, a cap, a fishing kit, a rifle, food, an emergency transmitter, and soap.
8. Brian may feel that it was too easy using them and that he liked relying on himself to get things done. (Answers may vary.)
9. Brian had left the transmitter on by accident.
10. The changes in Brian were that he had lost 17% of his body weight, he was more observant, more thoughtful, he was fascinated by food, and he had dreams.

Page 42—Unit Test: Option 1

True or False

1.T   2.F   3.F   4.F   5.T

6.F   7.T   8.F   9.F   10.T

Short Answer

1. Warmth, protection, cooking
2. He is injured by the quills. He learns to make fire.
3. Helpless
4. Events
5. Tired of light meat, wants variety.
6. The plane had flown off course.
7. Animals can't afford to play.
8. The moose, bear, tornado, etc.
9. A raft.
10. Accept any reasonable answers.

Essay: Accept any reasonable answer.